TOSSED LIKE WEEDS
FROM THE GARDEN

TOSSED LIKE WEEDS FROM THE GARDEN

HUGH MACDONALD

BLACK MOSS PRESS
1999

Published in October 1999 by Black Moss Press 2450 Byng Road, Windsor, Ontario N8W 3E8.

Black Moss books are distributed in Canada and the U.S. by Firefly Books, 3680 Victoria Park Ave., Willowdale, Ontario, Canada M2H 3K1. All orders should be directed there.

Black Moss Press would like to acknowledge the generous support given by the Canada Council for the Arts for our publishing program.

CANADIAN CATALOGUING IN PUBLICATION DATA

MacDonald, Hugh, 1945 —
   Tossed like weeds from the garden

Poems.
ISBN 0-88753 –330-2'

   1.   Title

PS8575.D6306T68 1999   C811'.54 C99-900737-8
PR9199.3.M2513T68 1999

FOR SANDRA

TABLE OF CONTENTS

CREAM

My cousin was sick and nine cows to be milked
one Hereford, one Jersey, and seven Holsteins
wide-bellied giants in a wide-bellied barn.
I was from the city, my hands small and white,
but I learned how to pinch a milk cow's teet
below the bulging udder, to sweep fingers top to tip
like falling dominoes, wring out a rivulet
of milk to shriek like a soprano
across the bottom of the galvanized pail
and rise squirt by squirt, bubbled to the rim.
I pinched the bucket between bony knees
swayed, narrow butt on one-legged stool
head buried in the sour bristle
of the old cow's side, right ear lashed
by her metronome of tail.
Behind me I heard the gush
propelled by Billy's calloused hands
and felt like a wee boy pissing
beside an uncle primed with beer.
The Jersey's large soft teets
fitted easily into my awkward hands
she was the only cow I'd ever milked.
But cousin Buddy lay sick upstairs in bed
and Billy'd finished three cows to my one.
My fingers ached and the muscles of my arms
felt stiff as steel, but I would do my best
and so I did with three before we quit
and tramped across the red clay yard
arms yanked towards the earth by near full pails,
past steamy kitchen heat to pantry's cool,
stretched fresh-scrubbed cheesecloth
across the separator's waiting bowl
lifted leaden buckets up and slowly poured,
filtered straw and seed from still-warm milk.
I strained to turn the counter-weighted arm
to overcome the stubborn slowness of the start
turned and turned and turned and turned until

it had no further need of help from me
and stopped the steady nagging of its bell
turned the tap beneath the brimming bowl
so milk fanned out upon the silver dome
seeped down inside a space where spinning discs
uncovered hidden fat and rose it up
to pour out thickly from the topmost spout
a creamy beige into a gallon jar
while from the lower nozzle blue-white skim
fell to a frothy pail upon the floor.
The buttery cream we poured into a can
we stored in shady coolness in the stream
then went by creeping train to Charlottetown
for cash to buy the things we couldn't grow.
The skim milk fed young cattle in the barn
and pigs that fought and snorted 'round their trough.

Grampy didn't have much time for boys
but that day he grinned and called me "quite a man."
The doctor'd been to visit while we milked.
My cousin's stuck in bed a few more days.
We spent another hour washing up
the separator, buckets and ourselves.
Grampy put a man-sized helping on my plate
though it was not food but happiness I ate
no one had ever told me what to do
down there they didn't have to, I just knew.

TOSSED LIKE WEEDS FROM THE GARDEN

I'll need the both of you
they've gotten right big, he says
and washes up his hands
in the chipped basin
next the kitchen pump.
Shoulda done them long ago
and you, young fella, Grampy looks at me,
you'll hafta watch yourself;
they've got sharp teeth, he says,
and hands us his things:
the Coca Cola bottle,
the milky gallon jar
of diluted Dettol,
the pocket knife
he sharpens,
shh, shh, on the steel.
And then side by side
like we belonged together
we stride to the pen
below the barn
and step inside.
The weiners lift their heads
and look at us,
crowd against the fence
in the farthest corner,
clear their throats
as if they knew
and Grampy's knife
whispers shh, shh, shh
against the steel
while Billy grabs the first
squee-eel, squee-eel, squee-eel,
drags him by the hind leg,
squee-eel, squee-eel, squee-eel,
rolls him on his back
take his legs like this, he says,
right hand, hind leg

left hand, front leg
cross hind with front.
Mind his teeth, my Grampy says,
right hand front leg,
left hand, hind,
and yank them together
just like Billy did.
And the pig clears his throat
and waits,
while grampy pours Dettol
inside the Coke bottle,
slices the scrotum
with his sharp knife,
squee-eel, 'squee-eel, squee-eel
the smell, the smell, the smell,
Grampy's fingers in the pig's bag
lift the pig's balls one at a time
slash, slash, slash, slash,
narrow things like chicken giblets
tossed like weeds from a garden,
pour in the Dettol,
squee-eel, squee-eel, squee-eel.
Oh how my arms ache,
I'm gonna throw up,
I say to myself
but can't let on.
Am I man or mouse?
Let go when I say, Billy says,
are you ready? Now!
I'll get the next one
and there are thirteen more
and then supper:
sausages...
and I have scrubbed,
and scrubbed, and scrubbed
the smell won't go,
my nose twitches.
What's the matter,
aren't you hungry? Grampy says.

GRAMPY'S WIRE MACHINE

We are fencing
Billy, Buddy and I
below the new barn
(Hurricane Hazel
took down the old one)
a new roll
of barbed wire
sits on the small trailer
behind the tractor
with a box of wire staples,
two hammers,
a wooden-handled wire stretcher,
round-pointed shovel,
a pile of sharpened juniper stakes,
and an eight pound maul.
The old fence wire
is rusted and brittle,
too old to be much use,
repaired too many times;
won't keep the cattle
off the roads
or from dying
of a bloated belly
full of rutabaga tops.
Buddy runs
the shovel handle
through a roll of wire.
Billy untangles a few feet,
holds the end against a post.
I drive home two staples
and Buddy walks
slowly backwards
laying out a careful line
on the ground before him.
Climb on the trailer, Billy says.
Let's get this done!

He starts the old Ford
and Buddy holds tight
as the razor-toothed roll
spins out along the fence
much faster than before
until tooth snags tooth,
and will not part,
yanks Buddy off the back,
shovel and spool of spiny wire
snatched from his hands.
Lord Sufferin' Moses, he yells
when he stops rolling
through hay and thistles.
Grampy materializes then and there
like a grumpy guardian angel.
That's no way to run wire...
Too dangerous, he says
through his bushy moustache,
We'll build something safer.
He walks toward the house
—and we wait and wait
hot and thirsty,
know it's a waste of time
but not worth arguing—
returns with a wooden machine,
designed on the spot,
a spindle in a box.
Nails it to the trailer floor,
loads in the wire
and stands aside.
Go ahead, he says.
At least you won't
rip your stupid arms off!
Billy climbs on the tractor,
Buddy sits on a mossy rock,
and I stand and wait,
sense it won't take long.
Grampy built the thing

from old barn boards
grey and dry and tired
with too much weather.
The tractor lurches off
pays out wire along the stakes
and Grampy walks to the house
whistling, smoke from his pipe
forming clouds of contentment
above his faded hair.
As his bent back
and worn sweater
disappear into the yard
the new wire snags
pulls old boards apart
and the roll jumps
through the air,
settles in a tangle
in the long grass by the fence.
Billy stops the tractor
backs it up again.
Buddy shrugs,
rises from the rock,
slips the shovel handle
back through the wire,
climbs on the trailer
and Billy pulls ahead...

OUTHOUSE

A winding path
cuts a red wound
up a grassy hill
a hundred feet
from the sway-backed house
to the weathered privy
a wooden closet
with a one-holed bench
and a single cob-webbed window
facing the grove.
The door stays closed
except for going in
or coming out.
There is no welcome mat
no room for dogs or pigs
at any time
or drifts of frosty snow
in icy winter.
It is a holy place
for blue-backed flies
and requires an act of faith
from any child
who trusts to sit
above such awesome waste
not knowing what lurks below
or what round cheeks
might press themselves
to the dusty window
or what eye
fills what crack
between what shrunken boards
or what ears hear what sounds.
There are catalogues to read
before they disappear
page by page
into the black hole

where they rattle
when pissed upon
like baseball cards
against bicycle spokes
and down there in the pit
a mountain of spicy logs
builds upwards to a peak.
We shovel in lime
to shrink it down
and cover up the stench
and once each summer
have to clean it out...
On my visits to the country
I got to know
more about life
than I really wanted to.

WALKING BETWEEN FIELDS

edging evergreen woods
my Grampy
picks and points
and I listen
more to the murmur
of his voice
than the import
of his words.
He names everything
plants, trees, animals,
insects, birds, fungi,
footprint, feather, rock,
talks of characteristics,
usefulness, dangers,
season, beauty,
nuisance and charm.
The sun shines warm
across our shoulders
birds serenade
and insects hum.
He tells me to remember
all he names
and I say I will...
I remember still
his softness of voice
the smell of his pipe
the shapes and colours
where we walked,
his guiding hand
and pointing finger,
but not a single word,
a solitary name.
I wish I did
and yet I know
now who I am,
and that
if I walked
with him again
I'd do the same.

FRESHENING

Nellie and Sarah
were "no spring chickens"
back in them times
when they bought
their first cow,
a young heifer
due to freshen
in the spring
and veterinarians
were scarcer than money.
So they called
my grandfather
on the old crank phone
one long and two shorts
and asked if he could come
over in the spring
when the calf was due.
They told him the date
the former owner
scratched on a shingle
with a rusty nail
and Grampy said he would.
Sure enough,
a few days before the date
he came over
and inspected the cow
told them what to look for
when the calf had dropped.
They called him every day
to say that nothing had changed
and one day to say it did.
On a chilly evening
just after supper
he knocked on their door
and they let him inside.
Should we boil some water? They asked

and he said, Yes...
and throw in some tea.
I like it strong
and a biscuit would be nice
with a bit of cheese.
And while it brewed
he went to check the cow
two anxious ladies
on his heels
and he came back
and asked for a fresh cup
and as the evening came
and more and more darkness
he sipped the tea
and read the paper
and every now and then
Nellie or Sarah or both
would scurry to the barn and back
and he just sat and sat.
The night was dark as pitch
when he next went out
and strolled to the barn
and this time he stayed
cursing from time to time
as he would when things went wrong.
Damn it all to hell! he cried
out of the darkness
in the barn.
What's wrong, Allister?
Sarah asked.
It's breech, he said,
I have to turn the little thing,
and there were grunts
and groans and curses.
And do you need a light? Nellie asked.
and Grampy laughed and cursed again.
Christ woman! he said,
I've got my hands in here,

not my head.
And the women walked to the house
worried and waited
until he kicked at the door
stood there grinning
holding the slippery calf
while Sarah fetched a lamp.

NIGHT VISITOR

Eleven years old
Grampy and Grammy,
Agnes and the boys
have gone to town.
I sit in the rocking chair
in the kitchen
of their old house
in Georgetown Royalty
a book in my lap
the nearest neighbour
miles away.
It's the first time
I've ever been
in such a place
so far from home
so far from anyone
but I told them all
I wouldn't be afraid,
that I'd be fine alone
and so I was
for quite a while
amid the shadows
and the deepening dark
but then the silence
of the empty house
begins to tinker
with my mind.
It's just the wind, I think
or just the creaking
of old timbers
the flap of loose shingle
the scurry of mouse
in the hollow walls
the tic, tic, tic,
of branches on glass.
It was nothing, I knew

but still the hair rose
behind my neck
and I began to sing
as loudly as I could
to cover up those sounds
but it was heard
outside in the night
and something crashed
against the door
and I ran to get the gun
but was too slow
the door swung wide
and with snort and grunt
the old sow walked inside
and I laughed
and chased her out
walking her to the barn.
I closed her in her pen
and stayed to chat
but didn't sing.
I fed her grain
and hung around
until I saw the headlights
of the Plymouth
swept the bottom
of the lane
and went inside
to wait.

SUNRISE WITH A TWIST

Morning meringue
on a lemon river
filters citrus sun

WILD GEESE

Sky sailors
stagger over oat stubble
laugh and shout like drunks

SPRING

White on white ground
under winter blankets
green dreams wait

AUTUMN AFTERNOON

Like ripe fruit
leaves rattle silently
outside my window

WHAT I CANNOT HAVE

I cannot feel
the sun behind a cloud
rain tastes of your tears

STORM SHELTER

Warm and delicious
pizza primavera
a safe harbour

UP IN THE AIR

Seven seagulls
float the updrafts.
Eight minds up in the air.

FEBRUARY 17, 1999

Five gull day, wind southwest.
The sun, whose fingers are icy,
has warm eyes.

THE PROBE IS TOO DEEP

the dental hygienist's hazel eyes
hide in the white forest
of my beard
reflected in the hovering mirrors
of her eye glasses.
Her microscopic scrutiny
and questions like:
> *Have you been flossing?*
> *Do you get the bristles of your brush*
> *into the crowns of those teeth?*

make me tell lies like a child.
But here in the chair
she has the power to probe
secrets hidden between teeth
buried below the borders of the gum line.
Today she falls silent
pulls and tears at my mouth
while I struggle not to wince.
When the probe is too deep
to dream away moments
of abraded and ripped flesh
I discover that her mind, too, wanders
the deep cavern of my dark mouth
when she says, bringing me to earth,
> *You wouldn't believe what I was dreaming about.*
> *I was at my funeral in a coffin.*
> *I dread that, you know. I'm worried about my hair*
> *and how I'll look, my makeup...*
> *I've no idea where a thought like that came from.*
> *Have you ever written a poem about going to the dentist?*

No, but perhaps I will, I say
because I suspect her musing's born
in the casual contemplation
of my gum disease.
She stops to rinse my mouth,
makes me bend my head

much farther than it wants to go,
jabs too deeply
around my back teeth,
peels flesh from bone,
jots numbers like class marks
on a rectangular report card,
> *That one's a six.*
> *Has Dr. MacDonald talked to you*
> *about periodontal surgery?*
I mumble yes he has;
recall stitches and swelling
in a friend's mouth.
> *Do you mind this very much?*
Still stinging from the insult
she doesn't know she gave
when my mouth turned her mind to death,
I contemplate revenge:
Perhaps, I say, this would be fun
if you wore black leather
and carried a long whip.
> *A dominatrix dental hygienist...*
She hesitates,
> *Let's not go there!*
For the next little while
she talks golf,
and summer plans,
just nervous small talk,
until the dentist comes to check my teeth
and she leaves the room.
She comes back for a moment
wearing her coat, ready for home.
> *If you write that poem*
> *I'd like to see it...*
> *To censor it...*

BANTAM

a breed of domestic fowl characterized by small size and pugnacity.
(Funk and Wagnalls Standard Dictionary)

Someone else's huge kid
wearing a black sweater
hovers near the blue line
like a murderous hawk.
My son glides
with the liquid ease
of non-checking hockey
learned at the Pee Wee level,
carving indelible lines
on his father's memory.
Now a Bantam he hesitates
takes a pass head down,
swoops like a swallow
delirious with sunlight
toward the opposing net.
The dark defenceman
drops from nowhere
slams him to the ice,
the explosion
of their contact
against the boards
echoes and rattles
round the rink.
He struggles for breath
fights the sense
of swallowed tongue,
weakness in the knees,
shrugs, sighs,
sets his teeth,
picks up his ruffled wings,
head high and proud,
and flies away.

OUTDOOR RINK

When Betty skates
at Holy Redeemer rink
under blushing
northern lights
that pulse
like the hearts
of red-cheeked boys
who swarm about her
like frenzied bees
around their queen
there I am between
her and them
my scrawny arms
stretched like toffee,
I, scarfed and hooded
in snowsuit armour
four years old
scrambling bent-ankled
on thin-skinned skates.
I learn to fly
like a snowflake
across knock-knee ice.
These are happy days
and though she smiles
at all the older guys
she tells them all
that I'm her only beau.

KITE DREAMS

I

a diamond of butcher-paper
on a cross of wood,
twelve paper bow ties
play follow-the-leader
like cans on a wedding car,
a spool
of butcher's twine
tied to the cross tree,
carried by a child
up the clay lane
to the hillock
in the heart
of the field
above the house.
Eyes uplift
heart already overhead.

KITE DREAMS

II.

The flying of kites
requires steady wind,
the courage
to run against the flow.
As the mind climbs,
hand binds
earth to sky
with simple string.
Barefoot child
on solid ground
mind's eye
a dance of faith
in azure sky.

THE OBJECT OF THE GAME

those brilliant afternoons
was to get Willy Edmonds
—dressed in his Sunday best—
close to a puddle,
toss the ball to him,
and bring him down.
If successful,
we'd stand around and laugh
as he limped away,
dripping and muddy,
toward his house
on Ambrose Street.
No one owned real gear,
sometimes we had a football,
but any ball would do.
Some guys would wear
their father's golf shoes
if the old man
wasn't out at Belvedere.
Those left tiny purple bruises
on our legs and backs.
One time
Danny lost his front teeth
on the steel horseshoe heel
of someone's army boots,
and one of the Doctor's boys
broke his leg.
We followed the doctor
along McGill Terrace
as he carried his son
down to his car
and watched them
drive off to the hospital.
Later we all signed the cast
but that game continued
as all those games did

in the days before helmets,
and I can't recall
any parent's fretting voice.

WILLIAM'S POEM

Clumps of matted grass
from fall's last mowing
lie like animal pelts
just beyond the chain-link fence.
Farther back a balding dogwood
clings to orange berries
amid a line of motley alder,
and back of that
the spartan bleakness
of a threadbare
trailor court.
My English class flees
with the alarm
of the noon bell,
like Fleance,
Banquo's pathetic cries
ringing in their ears.
The sky outside
—blued cotton
a bedsheet paled
from too much washing—
is cut by a single
arc of vapour trail
heading south
toward Louisiana
much like the marks
our children cut
in artificial ice
with skate blades
so proud fathers can dream.

UNDER THE CANNONS

Nobody told us
that the harbour
was a cesspool
in the days
when we propped
our bikes
against the cannons
of Fort Edward
and ran down
to the wooden-sided
bath-houses
across from the canteen
in Victoria Park.
We aimed
for high tide
when opaque water
lapped just below
our feet.
On muggy afternoons
boys in sagging woolen trunks
jumped and dove
from walkways
or fencetops
or ignored
the posted signs
and plunged in
from the roof.
The water touched
cool against summer skin
and we were laughingly alive.
My mother used to say:
You'll eat a peck of dirt
before you die,
so swallowing filthy water
seemed part of growing up,
like ear aches

and dysentry
and other summer ills.
But when my brother
got the fever
and his legs wouldn't move
our worried mother
phoned Doctor Frank
and thanks to that
his polio wasn't bad,
he never had a limp
or a leg brace
like so many others.
Today civil servants
and people with time
for fitness
walk the boardwalk
past the ghosts
of bathing houses
before which only sunlight
laughs on harbour water,
folks from the yacht club
sail there
all summer long,
but children don't swim
there any more.

SAILING WITH DAVID

Wind lifts the small
hairs on my neck
and lapping water
carves out room for thought
the sun soothes
and what words are spoken
are those required
to keep keel
above sand
and rock.
It is easier
to exist in silence
than in an avalanche
of sound.
And when you ask
what we talked about
I can remember more
from what was never spoken
than I can
from any sermon
I've ever heard.

THE BUCCANEERS

In this
their inaugural season
the Buccaneers
make eight first downs,
don't score a single point.
There are popped knees,
a broken jaw,
a dislocated shoulder.
They do laps and stretches,
crabwalks and monkey rolls,
pushups and sprints.
They practise and practise
lose game after game
but no one seems to care.
They make the playoffs
since there are only
four teams in the league.
October 31st rises up,
from three days of heavy rain,
Simmons Field is under water.
The semi-final game,
and David's father
comes to watch.
Seventeen boys
shiver through warm-ups,
run, tackle, and slide.
They lose thirty-five to nothing
don't make a single first down,
run off the field shivering,
like fresh dug potatoes
garnished in Island mud.
Next Sunday
it's the Lobster Bowl
and it's certain they'll lose.
But not before they've won.

SUMMERS FULL OF WARM DRIFTING

Inkerman P.E.I. July 1957

Bicycles sun bathe
in the rusty sand
catching their breaths
at the river's edge
while their master's
small behinds,
wedged
in black rubber doughnuts,
navigate their innertubes
in the warm water
off Inkerman.
Most of them can't swim,
and no one worries
about drifting out too far
or tumbling
from tired stretched latex
which might burst and spill
its rancid air.
They go home,
backs red as jellyfish,
wobble up
North River Road
towards McGill Avenue,
tubes over handlebars
burnt legs pump-pumping,
hunger gnawing
at their slender guts
aware only
of a tomorrow of summers
full of warm drifting.

STREET HOCKEY

McGill Avenue
didn't lend itself to street hockey
so we always ended up
in front of Jimmy Duffy's
on Highland Avenue one street down.
It was a good spot,
close to Highland Groceteria
to where runny-nosed boys
shuffled on hot, thirsty afternoons
for lime rickey or iron brew
with Island potato chips
and a paper bag of candy.
The game itself was a boy's game,
except when we let Snowball play
(the neatest girl in the whole neighbourhood
—she died of leukemia the next year)
with no divisions set up by age
but simply by whom we'd let play,
even some big boys without friends
who used their weight and size
to earn respect from us smaller guys.
And even fathers coming home
from work in suits and ties
would steal a moment
with some kid's borrowed stick
to have fun for a change.
No graceful glide on slick ice here
but feet solidly planted on hot asphalt.
No shin pads, just skinned knees
and ash or hickory on bone,
hip on hip, elbow in ribs, gut and face
and before long a real hockey fight,
no elegant dance behind padded gear
just bone on bone and blood for blood.
And every afternoon some cranky neighbour,
held up perhaps a minute on the street,

or hiding behind pinched Venetian blind,
would telephone cops who'd come up fast
like we were robbing some rich guy's house,
and ask names, and we'd give names,
—of kids we didn't like a few streets down,
their addresses and telephone numbers
carefully memorized and spat out when required.
Then they'd send us home
and we'd go away a few long minutes
until we saw them pass again,
and out we'd come and play some more.

A KISS LIKE HERS SHOULD NEVER HAVE AN END

I am lost, I am lost, in the robes of this light.

S. Plath

Even when we touch there is space between us.
Well-defined orbits make for a safe sky. I imagine
You and I separate particles, adrift on one small planet.
I'm never satisfied: I have no sense of shame.
Only fools sustain themselves on hopeless dreams.
In the season of asteroids, I long for meaningful collision.

And all of this from just one kiss: one New Year's Eve,
Warm wet lips. They've turned me from my course.
Cut loose from you I drift like black ice in space.
How thick and cold my blood's become.
Where are the shining eyes of God?
There is no light within such depthless dark.

If I can have you, then I'll gladly wait.
I'll let you live your days, I'll lurk outside. And so I sit
While others whirl you 'round and fill you up
Leave legacies of lies and drain your cup.
I'll settle for what's left when they are done. I know
How much of you there is. There'll be enough.

Mother of planets, only turn the sun on me!
I'll smile upon her face such loving light.
Make me shine. I will lighten up her steps.
We will whirl through space in endless dance.
And that will do just fine. How could I still want more?
Such bliss, such bliss, a kiss like hers should never have an end.

HEART'S BLOOD

Today I choose to rise and share
Your waking moments sleepy rose,
Your breath this morning rich and fair
A matins blessing for my nose.
My eyes view prismic beads of dew
Bright jewels on each fleshy flower,
And I am so in need of you
So deep in sleep at this green hour,
That I am moved to ply my art,
To work around each tender bud,
And touching every wilting part
Am born a brother in the blood,
Within your vestal crown of thorns
This sweetest yet of early morns.

LOVE YOU 'TIL I DIE

I love those moments
when your praying mantis
body craves nutrition
and I am victim
and victor in one.
You lie there
smiling in your sleep
and I your willing servant
come tender
to your bed.

SANCTUS

I remember: the open censer,
charcoal
glows white hot,
two silver spoons of incense
sprinkled,
clouds form
      and lift:
Et introibo ad altare dei
Ad Deum qui laetificat
juventutem meam
air alive with angels,
      sunbeams charged with dust.
Dandelions, buttercups,
black-eyed susan,
daisy and lilac,
the dancing stars
on the green harbour,
a baseball card
held by a clothespin
purrs like a cardboard cat
across bicycle spokes.
Twelve years old.
The fine hair
on the back of my neck
teased by passing wind.
Everything under the sun
or the moon whispers
one girl's name.
I am in love
with Linda's hazel eyes...

WHEN SUMMER COMES

back lit
by rising sun
every budded
tree and shrub
struts to show
the season's latest
shade of leaf.
Here and there
the spindly arms
of pin cherry
hold bright bouquets
like eager brides,
naked maples blush
amid lush,
verdant finery.
Brazen fields display
brash inflamed bosoms
through transparent coats
of virgin barley and oats
and from the fringe
of field and edge of wood
and all around
the fevered heat
of springtime rises up.
The powdered fern
uncoils its feathery frond.
Asparagus
thrusts forth
its braided glans.
Rhubarb
boldly parts
the dew damped grass
and I am moved
to think of you
while summer's warm breezes
whisper promises in my ears.

IN A CONCH SHELL

The memory
of a long abandoned sea,
resonant echoes
of a cathedral cavern
reverberating cannon
of the sea cave
sunrise riding
on the pounding surf
hum of distant highways,
overhead wires
the childhood whispering
of children grown and gone
the wind among pines
the gentle breathing
of a loved one
sinking softly into sleep

HALLOWEEN POEM

He sits on her kitchen floor
his insides strewn
across the sports pages
mouth a toothy grin
eyes dull and listless.
Inside his head
nothing but hope,
a dream of hands
lighting a candle
and placing it inside.

REFLECTIONS ON LAURIE'S POEM
WHILE SUPERVISING FINAL EXAMS

January 25, 1997.

She wrote a poem
about being in love
with a man
who knew her well
enough to understand
all her colours,
about fitting together
like a jigsaw,
her breasts
finding the soft place
under his ribs,
how bad it feels
to discover
one piece
in the heart
of the puzzle is absent,
how it feels
to take apart all those pieces,
and toss them
back into the box
with the picture she dreamed
on its cover
where she will write
piece missing
just as a reminder.

PLACES

Let's try not to utter empty words
they lack even simple music.

In those last hours her eyes were whirlpools.
I think she's looking at me, my sister said, and I don't know what
to do.

In her house are quiet places where no demons hide.
But everywhere the hands of the clock turn, the vice pinches.

My heart is a bird in a rusting cage.
There is no sanctuary even in safe places.

Your joy comes lately with a tidy house.
In nature grass grows long and dust covers everything.

FOURTEEN

She and I were walking
and we came
to the stump of an elm
in a clearing
and beside it
a clump of burdocks
and she went
to the stump
which was damp
and covered
in black slime mould
and she sat there
talking to me
as if she didn't care
about her skirt
as if she didn't know
I could hardly speak
because of how she looked
in that sweater.

FOR LINDA AND LAURIE
AND THE UNKNOWN NAKED WOMAN
IN THE GLOBE AND MAIL

Last night I can't sleep
your poem flickers
inside my dark mind
like electric lights in a blizzard,
images like colour slides
appear and disappear:

That woman's ecstatic face,
her naked photo taking half the page,
arms spread wide like a crucifix
jagged line indenting half her chest,
the sculpted perfection
of her remaining breast
tattooed flowers near the wound
sign of a soul determined
to paint joy even on scars.

How blessed, I think
are the lovers of women,
the Samuel Hollands of inner walls,
tasters of unbidden droplets,
gardeners of hollyhocks and roses,
connoisseurs of brown berries,
turners of dials,
explorers of those inside spaces
that hold poems, babies
and so much joy.

LOVE'S CONSTRUCT

Love constantly constructs
its own dimensions,
and love's construction
destroys existing structures
and with old love's debris
builds new walls.
Warm lips seek willing lips
and mouths the taffy touch
of salt-sweet tongues,
breasts the compress
of opposing breasts,
flesh, the soothing press
of silken skin,
hands the rolling hills
of human landscape,
ears scan the atmosphere
for the music of certain voices
eyes link to beckoning eyes
like burdocks to wool.

ETERNALLY OLENKA

Like the surface of water,
some moments hold a delicious tension.
That evening at the Westerner Motel
when he washed Olenka's hair,
he stood behind her shirtless back
admiring the curve of her neck,
the unfamiliar physics of her brassiere.
She likely sensed the changes in him,
the rapid throb of certain veins,
an involuntary tremor in lathered fingers
or the tangle of distracted thoughts
expressed in speech.
It occurred to him that she expected him to take
the opportunity to free her pent-up breasts
from the lace-trimmed fabric he pretended
to ignore as she slipped the sweater over her head,
to feel their fleshy substance warm his hands
and fill his mind with ravenous dreams,
their heft outweighing earthly care.
But for some reason he cannot remember,
whether cowardice or wisdom,
he decided to remember her just like this,
trusting him, half-dressed in a motel bathroom,
with shampoo in her hair...

SHAPE SORTER

Wave upon relentless wave
chases itself
onto Souris Beach,
collapses and glides
upon the belly
of whirling sand.
The wind spits
past its teeth,
breath menthol cool
and clean.
On Main Street
he ignores the whine
of tires on pavement
the moan
of overhead wires,
sinks inside himself
under a liquid sea of air,
feels her lithe form
ride across him
like crashing surf
shaping and reshaping
the sandy shores
of his lonely island
until he no longer
recognizes himself.

BLACK IRON

The best time
to black the kitchen range
is when no coals groan
and crackle in the box,
for even heat-resistant paint
needs time to mature
and even so
the first new fire
fouls household air
a little while.
      But I know you,
how you'll like the way
polished chrome
looks against black iron
and how refurbished metal
seems more able
to purge the chill
from cold bones.

FIRE AND RAIN

In the morning the fire is down to glowing coals
you bring fresh kindling and I open the drafts.

Those who love us overlook our flaws,
the undertaker will make us young again.

In the winter the roads are covered in ice,
but the ditches fill with snowy pillows.

Neither the red petals of roses nor your warm blood
can grow a heart in a mannequin.

Snow is the frozen fingerprint of the rain,
it paints a cleansing white across the blemished fields

TROPHIES

She says the poems will not come,
too many doors have locks, too many windows shutters.

It was all a mistake you know,
When I fell in love with her, I thought she was someone else.

In the upturned faces of her children, there is a glimpse of God,
but they still have much to learn.

Her house is shingled in steaming yellow pancakes,
her fingers fat sausages sweet with spice.

All of her walls are hung with trophies of his kills,
she pretends he's put them there to watch her.

GUIDED MEDITATION

Warm words
set my scalp afloat,
fluid fingers
that soothe
the tender places
within my mind.
They dance
like gasoline fumes
around the open flame
of a ravenous soul,
drawn like feathery moths
to any spark they find
upon a darkening earth.
And yet I sense her fear
imagine lines of scars
beneath the green silk
of her blouse,
the nervous uncertainty
behind exploration of soul,
heard in the nervous lisp
of her moist tongue.
She dances around me
like a patient boxer,
seeks an opening,
wants to fit me
between the pages
of some book she's read,
a man like all the others
easily explained and understood,
then discarded
in the book burning
that is sexual politics.

HYMN

— for E.D.

Some days this world can be such hell
light years away from Heaven,
A vale of tears where sorrows dwell,
Black bread with little leaven.

It seems I have no say in this
I'm forced to bide my time,
And take the spittle with the kiss,
Cacophony with rhyme.

And when it is my day to die
My eyes smoke-glazed and blind,
Will angels bear me up on high,
Or leave me lost, behind?

THE VOICE OF GOD

I can find music
in the rain upon
the church roof
or battering the leaves
of the trees
along the street
and although the sun
outside cannot sing,
blessed by its heat
birds make melody
and the wind
absorbs its rays
and whistles,
rides past places
where aspens
rake brushes
over leafy snares.
But the rays that filter
past stained glass
upon some smug preacher
on a holy high horse
whose words
come hard and cold
like something dead
and in a tomb
accomplish nothing.
I close my mind
and await
the voice of god
in the swell of organ,
and heavenly anthems
born in a human soul.

SACRED SPACE

In the beginning
she says
she's not afraid to die:
If there's nothing there,
I won't know about it.
If there is, I'll be all right too.
Yet I'm not so sure
she's unafraid.
I recognize the symptoms.
I, too, sought certainties
and was afraid.
She wants to know
unknowables.
Her voice breaks
as she discusses
her sacred space,
how she doesn't always go there
but needs to know
it exists.
We sit
in awkward circles
in a dark basement.
She lights candles
joyful like the altar boy
I once was,
her sibilant voice
casts soothing spells.
I try to float
inside words warmed
and flavoured
by her mouth,
try but cannot
isolate words
from speaker.
My neck stiffens
in the wooden rocker

I shift about,
mind wanders,
remembers
the agnostics prayer:
O, God (if there is a god)
save my soul (if I have a soul)
and I peek
through partly-closed lids
into her expectant eyes
and shiver.

IN OUR HOUSES

wooden crosses
with white metal saviours
nailed hand and foot,
head punctured and bleeding,
pleading eyes
turned to a firmement
replaced in textbooks
by an ever expanding universe,
slices of dusty palm frond
tucked behind calenders,
luminous icons
in glass domed grottos
glow a nuclear green
in darkened bedrooms,
where only one
of the ghosts
was holy.

RANT

This morning
since I had no passengers
on my drive to work
I listened to Handel
played on an organ
in a rural church
somewhere in England

and then on a harp
in a castle in Wales.

It was that lovely,
empty-headed
emotional
sort of spiritualism
that lacks
the misdirected
pseudo-intellectualism
of fuzzy headed bishops.

There should be churches
where nothing but swell music happens

If we could just come to church
sing and play
and then go out
and be decent and fair

no more posturing
no more manipulation
of questionable scriptures
canonized by politicians
for politicians
who have
generation after generation
rationalized their right

to grow fat and lazy
in large stone buildings
while the same suffering
that plagued the earth
since humanities arrival on it
continues unabated.

OUTSIDE MY WINDOW

on the untrimmed lawn
the dandelions
wear parkas
with fur-fringed hoods.
They are scattered
like a motley army
beyond the wire-mesh fence.
Yesterday
their manes
were golden
and mine
a reddish-brown.
Time consumes colour
but dreams
are patient, youthful things
that grasp the slightest breeze,
lift and float away
on silken parachutes.

FIRE AND ICE

Three teen-age boys
lug newspaper,
kindling wood,
and stove-length maple
down to the river,
walk on top
like that fisher, Jesus,
—not a big deal
on a February night
at this latitude—
clear a patch
of surface snow,
voices steaming
like travelling Innu
chasing caribou
across tundra.
From a cardboard box
they draw skewers
and red ketchup,
roast chicken wieners
above the dancing fire,
eat them wrapped
in toasted bread,
dripping red paste,
while worshipping
town lights
in the distance
and stars overhead
dance and reel
across the ice.
In the morning
passing children will discover
the dark stain
of a hunter's fire
and scattered traces
of a recent kill

upon the trampled snow.
On the weekend
fresh snow sifts
temporary sediment
on fossils doomed
by spring
to melt into the river
of memory, speculation
and poetry.

MUSINGS ON CHOLESTEROL

My veins
are a river system
polluted by the world
wherein they flow,
where creatures
of diverse origin and colour
populate the shores
some indigenous
to the geography,
a few who have entered
by invitation,
occasional invaders
involved in guerrilla warfare
against the governing forces.
The waters
which began their days
as unpolluted
as a mountain spring
with the passage of time
have become overburdened
with siltation and effluviums
some planetary in origin,
some born of inappropriate choices,
some debris of the battlefield,
the pollutants of industry,
the striving after fame,
accumulation or lesser gain.
Inevitably the burden
of all this flotsam
proves too much for the struggling river
is dropped along the way
and over time, passages narrow,
so that the river flows inevitably
drop by drop to an ocean of darkness

ISLAND LIFE?

the old farmer repeated,
that's easy b'y.
We hibernate all winter
then work all summer
while you tourists
come over here
and scare the cows,
stir up dust
on the road
visitin' places around here
me and the wife
have never had time to see,
buyin' crafts
from a guy
in a Hawaiian shirt
who moved here
by mistake one summer
when it didn't rain
every day,
goin' to the theatre
at "Conflouridation" Centre
as if that operation
had anything to do
with the Island.
If you want to see
the real thing
you ought to go
on the pogie
and sit
in a draughty old house
watchin' the soaps
or go down to the Legion
some Friday afternoon
with your hat on
and buy us all a round
and then come home

and help me clean the barn
or go out with Joe
there, in early May
and help pull traps
or help me plant
some crops
'cause all that lobster
and all them colours
in them fields
didn't get there
by themselves
by Jesus!

THE INHERITANCE OF SCARS

What thoughts walk lost in the maze that's your mind?
What dreams are adrift in the gathering dark
never to be perused by light of day.
Your disembodied voice makes plaintive call
and casts about its carpe diem spell,
that hints at how it hurts to be alone.

So often I've preferred to be alone,
to sense the seamless pleasures of the mind,
to weave some lovely lies a little spell
—bright fibres warping patterns through the dark—
completely unaware that time would call
an end to all this magic one dread day.

One photo shows a far, far brighter day,
your eyes intent upon my face alone,
though likely we both heard my father call
for us to smile and if we did not mind,
he'd take one more in case the first was dark,
and his dear voice just fortified the spell.

When I was young you taught me how to spell,
to know the joys of reading every day,
of drawing near the lamp when it grows dark.
I loved those moments that I spent alone
and I got used to living in my mind
where I had myriad friends on whom to call.

O, how our dreams were dashed by one phone call.
How great the change that Alzheimer's would spell,
the grief of watching as you lost your mind.
You gave up playing mother on that day
to wander neural dungeons all alone,
to learn the world as sinister and dark.

And here I stand with one foot in that dark
and fear it won't be long until you call.
That's why I no longer wish to be alone,
am afraid I'll find a word I cannot spell.
I never want to let go of a day
or for a single moment close my mind.

           * * *

With those things on my mind I'll meet the dark
but while it's day I'll thankfully recall
our good times for a spell, and carry on alone.

MY MOTHER'S LAST WORDS
IN A CONVERSATION WITH HERSELF
EARLY DECEMBER, 1996.

Poppa, my Mommy
O God, my memory is short.
Will someone watch me?
Why is she looking for Aletha?
I don't know Momma,
I can't get it down.

Poppa, Poppa answer me.
I can't answer you
when I can't hear you.

Momma, Momma my angel
come to me
Holy Mary, mother of God.

I want something.

But you don't know how
to ask for it.
I can't ask the woman,
she's on mission.

MOTHER'S WAKE

—January 1997

people shuffle by
the brass frame
on the golden easel,
see your face
captured in black and white
hand coloured
frozen at twenty,
skin pinch-blushed.
And younger photos
you beside Reg,
your proud husband,
then holding three babies
and then their babies
on the bottom row.
In the polished box,
the face the undertaker
gave you
based on the snapshot
he found near your bed.
The people are in lines,
they pause to clasp and hug,
and talk of love
with their eyes,
murmur and grunt,
while in my mind
I watch the replay
of your slow death,
your chiselled features
shrink minute by minute
into the shrunken head
we played with as children
on the green linoleum
while you kneaded our bread.

WHEN YOU LOOK AT HER

At my age, he said
I can tell you
that when you look at her
you ought not to see her
as she is,
rather
as she will be
years from now.
Someone once told me
that when you find
a beautiful woman
you should follow her home
and ask to see her mother
because you'll be living
with her mother soon.
A man must consider the future
because that's where he will live.
Too many men marry dreams
discovered in the perfection of now,
and when the future does come
they are taken by surprise

ARRIVAL IN GOOSE BAY-HAPPY VALLEY

November 20, 1997

We land in the dark
fourth airport of the day
stand surrounded
by strangers from the plane
load suitcase and gear
into Tim's battered yellow van
(haven't met Tim yet)
overhead the stars startle
like sun polished diamonds set in tar
the outside air
swallows deep and cold
into the lungs
like spring water
in a mentholated throat.
The porous van
is punctured by frost
and smells of spent fuel
but the conversation
is a warm blanket
and laughter
bonds like crazy glue.
First stop the Moravian Church
an art show
a leafy forest
of hanging silk
with mountain ranges for walls
purple skies and deep cool lakes.
We leave our coats in the chapel
already at home.

ENTROPY

One news story says
that the extended eye
of humankind
bulges beyond
the extremities
of our solar system.
It falls upon
an errant planet,
the gravity of whose sun
proves insufficient
to hold its mass
in obedient orbit.
And so,
one lost planet,
through no fault
outside its own design,
careens toward
a rendezvous
with inevitable destruction.
On the same newscast
we hear about
Phil Hartman
whose wife's entropic reaction
to his proposed flight from orbit
leaves two young children
lost moons
cast adrift without planet or sun...

ERASING GRANITE

My father taught school
in the days
when another job
was needed to support the habit.
He drove the Island
evenings and weekends
selling bibles and religious goods
to the living,
and for the dead,
polished memorials
in granite and marble
or the dull green face
of lowly limestone
sandblasted to order.
He took orders
printed the names
neatly and carefully
never making a mistake,
—knowing that words
blasted into stone
endure for centuries—
until his father died.
Just this once
—emotion must have overcome him—
his printing was unclear
his "A" looked like an "S"
to the sandblaster
and so his father,
James A. MacDonald,
Jimmy Johnny Angus
of Donaldston, PEI
lies for as much of eternity
as black Vermont granite will allow
in a tiny cemetery
under a tombstone
that tells the world
"here lies
James S MacDonald."

SOOT ON FROST

Last night's flue fire
only a memory
its locomotive roar
tracking up the snapping pipe
into the pitch black frosty night
soot litters the crusty deck
a negative of snow flakes
on dark autumn wood.

GULL HOUSE

Most days
gulls line the roof ridge
spaced like wino's teeth.
The air alive
with their laments.
In the distance
down past Main
the harbour roils
and splashes
empty of boats
for the winter.
Inside the house
the television
blinks and flashes
across the silent room,
while the old fisher sleeps
on the red velour couch,
dreams of pulling nets
full of cod and hake,
and the laughing farm girl
waiting back on shore
with soft enticing eyes
in a loft of clover hay.

POEMS

Sometimes they grow in me silently
until they loom too large to contain
and they want out. They wake me up
in the middle of the night or make me
pull over to the side of the road
and write down their address
on the side of my coffee cup.
They climb like ragged vines
out of my heart, my mouth, my eyes,
my ears, my nose, my privates
and I try to fit them
along a left hand margin
of however many pages it takes.
And I can spend days trimming
and shaping a garden full of them
before I invite a friend to tea.
Sometimes poems are delivered to my door like milk
or they are pointed out
by small children who still have eyes for magic.
Sometimes I'm saying a poem
and don't know until another poet tells me so.
Poems get written by accident by people
who could never write one on purpose
and if you find one of those it's yours.
Sometimes I write a poem
to slow the passage of time
or as a time machine
to draw me back to that special place
whose memory has smouldered
in that part of the belly
where funny feelings dwell.
Sometimes I use someone else's form
like a bucket to fill.
Sometimes everything comes spilling out
and takes the shape of the place where it lands.
Other poems just sit around

and wait for me to come along,
hoping I'll be smart enough to recognize them.
I know they're always there
but too often I miss them
because my poem sense is overburdened
by the dark cloak of unimportant things.

THE MISTS DISSOLVE

Walking late last night
a chilling mist afloat
before the moonlit horizon,
slightly frightened
of the inherent danger
of my ardent solitude,
spooked by nature's shadows,
my heart gripped
in angina's fist.
Overhead an ant trail
of flashing aircraft
blinks toward Europe,
perhaps for a confrontation
with Serbian tragedy,
in their background
the sky's brilliant clockwork.
I am curiously comforted,
the mists dissolve
into icy nothingness
as I pass through them
and stride painlessly home
blood pumping boldly
past all obstructions.